Katherine HENGEL

# Cool
# CARROTS

## from
## Garden to Table

### How to Plant, Grow, and Prepare Carrots

A Division of ABDO
**ABDO**
Publishing Company

# visit us at www.abdopublishing.com

Published by ABDO Publishing Company, a division of ABDO, P.O. Box 398166, Minneapolis, Minnesota 55439. Copyright © 2012 by Abdo Consulting Group, Inc. International copyrights reserved in all countries. No part of this book may be reproduced in any form without written permission from the publisher. Checkerboard Library™ is a trademark and logo of ABDO Publishing Company.

Printed in the United States of America, North Mankato, Minnesota
102011
012012

PRINTED ON RECYCLED PAPER

Design and Production: Anders Hanson, Mighty Media, Inc.
Series Editor: Liz Salzmann
Photo Credits: Aaron DeYoe, Shutterstock. Photos on page 5 courtesy of  W. Atlee Burpee & Co. and Kitazawa Seed Co.

The following manufacturers/names appearing in this book are trademarks: Gold Medal Flour®, Kraft®, Arm & Hammer®, Market Pantry®, Roundy's®, Zatarain's®, Hellman's®, Crystal Sugar®, Michael Graves Design®, Pyrex®, The Pampered Chef®

**Library of Congress Cataloging-in-Publication Data**

Hengel, Katherine.
  Cool carrots from garden to table : how to plant, grow, and prepare carrots / Katherine Hengel.
     p. cm. -- (Cool garden to table)
  Includes index.
  ISBN 978-1-61783-183-6
  1. Carrots--Juvenile literature. 2.  Cooking (Carrots)--Juvenile literature.  I. Title.
  SB351.C3H46 2012
  635'.13--dc23
                        2011037250

## Safety First!
*Some recipes call for activities or ingredients that require caution. If you see these symbols, ask an adult for help!*

**Sharp** - *You need to use a sharp knife or cutting tool for this recipe.*

**Hot** - *This recipe requires handling hot objects. Always use oven mitts when holding hot pans.*

# CONTENTS

# WHY GROW YOUR OWN FOOD?

Because then you get to eat it, of course! You might not be the biggest carrot fan in the world. But have you ever had fresh carrots? Straight from your very own garden? If not, prepare to be surprised. Fresh food tastes wonderful!

Plus, fresh food is really healthy. All produce is good for you. But produce that comes from your own garden is the very best. Most folks do not use chemicals in their home gardens. That makes home gardens better for you and the **environment**!

Growing your own food is rewarding. All it takes is time, patience, soil, water, and sunshine! This book will teach you how to grow carrots in **containers**. Once they're ready, you can use them in some tasty recipes!

# CARROTS

Carrots are a root vegetable. They have been around for centuries! Carrots are a member of the parsley family. The parsley family also includes things such as dill, celery, and parsnips.

There are many kinds of carrots. Carrots can be white, yellow, orange, light purple, deep red, and even black! The shape varies from short stumps to thin cones. Each looks, tastes, and grows differently.

Nantes carrots are shaped like **cylinders**. They are orange and rounded at both ends. Nantes carrots are tender and sweet. Plus, they grow well in **containers**. Let's get started!

## TYPES OF CARROTS

| NANTES | ATOMIC RED | DANVERS | LUNAR WHITE | SOLAR YELLOW | PURPLE DRAGON |

# GROWING

In this book, you'll learn how to grow carrots in a **container** garden. With container gardens, you have more control over things such as light and temperature. But keep in mind that carrots grow differently in every climate.

## When to Plant

Go online to find out the average date of the last frost in your area. **Sow** your carrot seeds about two weeks before this date.

## The Right Conditions

### Sunlight
*Plants need sunlight to grow. Carrots need at least six hours of sunlight a day.*

### Pests and Weeds
*Be earth-friendly! Soap and water sprays keep pests away. White vinegar is a great weed killer.*

### Temperature
*Once carrot seeds **sprout**, the ideal temperature is 60 to 70 **degrees**. If it's hotter or cooler than that, bring the container inside.*

### The Right Soil
*Light, sandy soils work best. Heavy, crusted-over soil can prevent carrots from sprouting. Use soil rich in organic matter. This will help your plant hold moisture.*

# SOW YOUR SEEDS

**1**     **2**     **3**

## MATERIALS NEEDED

10-inch deep container with drainage hole

soil

water

carrot seeds

① Fill the **container** three-quarters full of soil. Wet the soil thoroughly.

② Sprinkle the carrot seeds over the soil. You'll thin the plants later, so don't worry about how the seeds are spaced.

③ Lightly cover the seeds with ¼ inch (.6 cm) of dirt. Water lightly.

4 Carrot seeds **germinate** in soil that is 50 to 70 **degrees**. If your climate is too warm or cold, start your seeds inside.

# STAGES OF

## Watering

Carrots need **consistent**, even watering. Stick your finger in the soil to check the moisture. Add water if the top 4 inches (10 cm) of the soil is dry.

## Thinning

Thinning means getting rid of a few plants so others have room to grow. You will need to thin your carrots twice. Use scissors to cut away some of the **seedlings** just below the soil. Do not pull the plants out of the soil. That could **disturb** the roots of the other plants.

THIN the carrots when the tops are 2 inches (5 cm) high. There should be 1 inch (3 cm) between each carrot.

FERTILIZE when the tops are 4 inches (10 cm) high.

WATER the carrots when the top 4 inches (10 cm) of soil is dry.

# GROWTH

## Fertilizing

**Fertilizer** has **nutrients** that help plants grow. It comes in pellets, powder, or liquid. It's often mixed with water. For carrots, use only one-half the **recommended** amount. Pour the fertilizer mix at the base of the plant, not over the leaves.

## Harvesting

Harvest the carrots when they are about ½ inch (1 cm) wide. You'll see bright orange "carrot shoulders" sticking out of the ground! Harvest early for sweet, tender carrots. Leave the harvesting until later if you prefer large, heavier carrots.

FERTILIZE again when the tops are 6 inches (15 cm) high.

THIN the carrots again when you see orange roots. There should be 3 inches (8 cm) between each carrot.

HARVEST them when they are about ½ inch (1 cm) wide.

9

# HARVESTING

## CARROTS

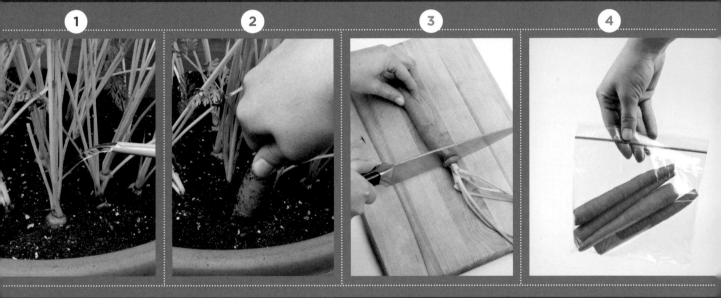

① Before harvesting, **soak** the soil around the carrots with water.

② Use a garden fork or trowel to loosen the soil around the plant. Then twist the tops while pulling up.

③ Cut the tops off as soon as the carrots are out of the ground.

④ Wash the carrots and put them in plastic bags. Do not peel the carrots until you are ready to use them! Keep the carrots in the refrigerator.

# Carrot Q&A

QUESTIONS & ANSWERS

### How Come My Seeds Didn't Sprout?

You should see **sprouts** within two to three weeks. Be patient! Sometimes carrot seeds can't sprout because the soil above them is too heavy, crusted, or hot.

### How Long Will it Take?

Carrots take 60 to 70 days to **mature**. But growth has a lot to do with the sun and temperature.

### How Do I Stop the Green Shoulders?

When the tops of carrots are above the soil line, they turn green. Covering the carrot "shoulders" with soil stops this problem.

### Why Are My Carrots Twisted Around Each Other?

Carrots twist when they are too crowded. That's why thinning is important. Twisted carrots are still tasty. They just look funny!

### What's With the Split or Hairy Carrots?

Not watering properly can make carrots split or grow hairy roots. Water carrots **consistently** and evenly.

# Cool Ingredients

**ALL-PURPOSE FLOUR**

**BAKING POWDER**

**BAKING SODA**

**BAY LEAVES**

**BREAD CRUMBS**

**BROWN SUGAR**

**BUTTER**

**CHICKEN BROTH**

**COLBY CHEESE**

**EGGS**

**FENNEL SEEDS**

**FRESH BASIL**

**FRESH DILL**

**GARLIC**

**GROUND CINNAMON**

**HALF-AND-HALF**

## HELPFUL TIP

*Carrots come in all different sizes, even if they are the same kind! Some recipes call for large carrots. In general, that means a carrot that is 6 to 8 inches (15 to 20 cm) long. If your carrots are smaller, just add a few more than the recipe calls for!*

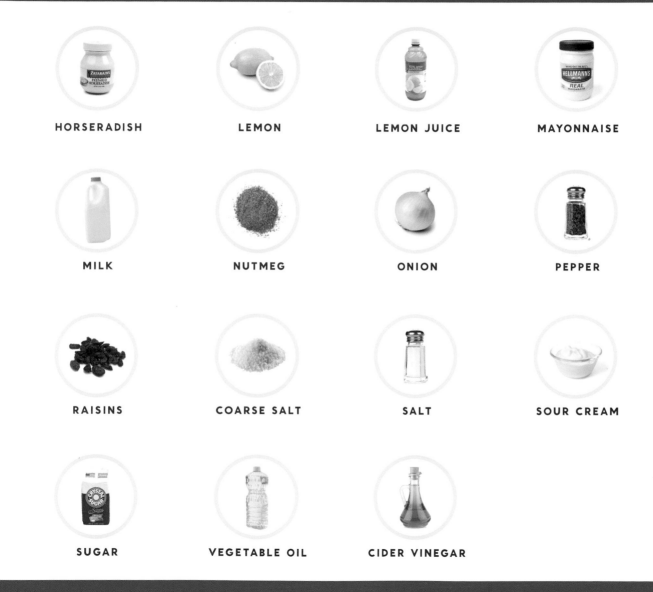

**HORSERADISH**      **LEMON**      **LEMON JUICE**      **MAYONNAISE**

**MILK**      **NUTMEG**      **ONION**      **PEPPER**

**RAISINS**      **COARSE SALT**      **SALT**      **SOUR CREAM**

**SUGAR**      **VEGETABLE OIL**      **CIDER VINEGAR**

# Kitchen Tools

**12-MUFFIN TIN**

**8×8-INCH BAKING DISH**

**BLENDER**

**CUTTING BOARD**

**FUNNEL**

**GARLIC PRESS**

**GRATER**

**LADLE**

**LARGE POT**

**MEASURING CUPS**

**MEASURING SPOONS**

**MEDIUM-SIZED POT**

{ **FAST FACT** }

*Carrots were first **cultivated** in and around Afghanistan. They grew purple carrots and yellow carrots. These carrots were brought to Europe in the tenth century. The orange carrot was bred in the Netherlands in the 1500s.*

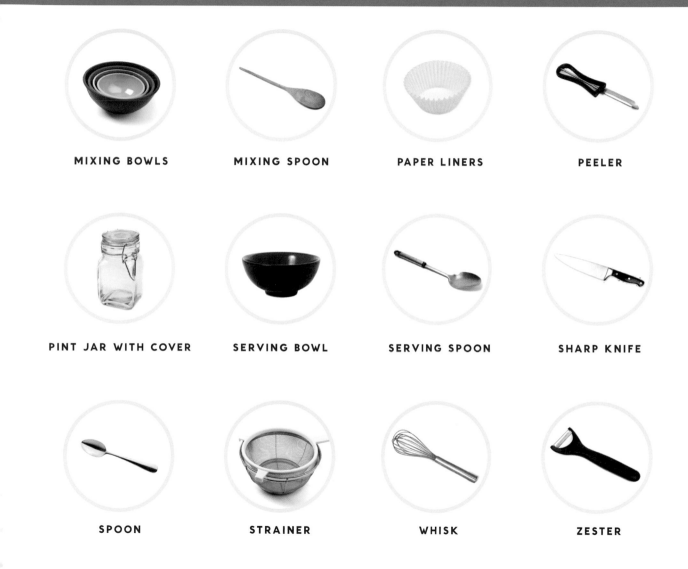

**MIXING BOWLS**    **MIXING SPOON**    **PAPER LINERS**    **PEELER**

**PINT JAR WITH COVER**    **SERVING BOWL**    **SERVING SPOON**    **SHARP KNIFE**

**SPOON**    **STRAINER**    **WHISK**    **ZESTER**

# Cooking Terms

### Fold

*Fold* means to mix ingredients by gently lifting and turning.

### Peel

*Peel* means to remove the skin, often with a peeler.

### Press

*Press* means to push an ingredient, often garlic through a garlic press.

### Grate

*Grate* means to shred something into small pieces using a grater.

### Slice

*Slice* means to cut food into pieces of the same thickness.

## Toss

*Toss* means to turn ingredients over to coat them with seasonings.

## Whisk

*Whisk* means to beat quickly by hand with a whisk or a fork.

## Zest

*Zest* means to lightly remove some of the peel from a **citrus** fruit using a zester.

### LENGTHWISE OR CROSSWISE

*To cut something lengthwise means to cut along its length. You create pieces that are the same length as the original.*

*To cut something crosswise means to cut across its length. The pieces will be shorter, but the same width as the original.*

# CHILLY

# Dilly Carrot Dip

### The best thing to happen to carrots since thinning!

## INGREDIENTS

1 garlic clove

4 sprigs of fresh dill

½ teaspoon salt

¼ teaspoon pepper

12 ounces sour cream

¼ cup mayonnaise

carrots for dipping

## TOOLS

garlic press

cutting board

sharp knife

measuring spoons

measuring cups

mixing bowl

mixing spoon

serving bowl

peeler

1. Press the garlic and chop the dill.

2. Put the garlic, dill, salt, pepper, sour cream, and mayonnaise in a mixing bowl. Mix well.

3. Put the dip in a smaller serving bowl. Put it in the refrigerator for at least one hour.

4. Peel the carrots. Cut off the ends. Cut the carrots in quarters lengthwise.

5. **Garnish** the dip with some fresh dill. Serve it with the fresh carrot sticks.

### Even Cooler

*This dip is great with any kind of veggie! Try celery, cucumbers, or tomatoes. It's great with chips or pita bread too!*

19

# PICKLED
# Carrot Sticks

Cucumbers aren't the only veggies that taste great pickled!

MAKES 1 PINT

## INGREDIENTS

4 to 6 carrots,
peeled

1 cup cider vinegar

¼ cup sugar

2 garlic cloves,
pressed

1½ teaspoons
fennel seeds

1½ tablespoons
coarse salt

2 bay leaves

## TOOLS

medium-sized pot

cutting board

sharp knife

strainer

pint jar with cover

measuring cups

measuring spoons

ladle or
canning funnel

peeler

grater

1. Bring a medium-sized pot of water to a boil. In the meantime, make the carrot sticks. Remove the ends of the carrots. Cut the carrots lengthwise. Then cut the carrots crosswise into thirds. This leaves six pieces per carrot. Cut the bigger pieces lengthwise again. They should all be about the same width.

2. Put the carrots in the boiling water. Simmer for one minute. Pour them into a strainer and rinse under cold water. Strain thoroughly. When the carrots are cool, put them in the jar.

3. In the same pot, heat the vinegar, sugar, garlic, fennel seeds, salt, bay leaves, and 1¼ cup water. When it begins to boil, reduce the heat and simmer for two minutes.

4. Remove the pot from the heat. Cool until room temperature. This is the brine. Use a ladle or a canning funnel to put the brine in the jar. Cover the jar and chill in the refrigerator for at least one day.

21

# CREAMY

# Carrot Soup

This amazing soup is so creamy it's dreamy!

MAKES 6 SERVINGS

## INGREDIENTS

8 large carrots, peeled and sliced

1½ cups chicken broth

2 garlic cloves, pressed

zest from 1 whole lemon

1½ cups half-and-half

2 tablespoon lemon juice

¼ teaspoon nutmeg

salt and pepper to taste

fresh basil

## TOOLS

peeler

cutting board

sharp knife

measuring cups

garlic press

zester

large pot

mixing spoon

blender

measuring spoons

ladle

serving bowls

① Put the carrots, chicken broth, garlic, and lemon zest in a large pot. Bring to a boil. Reduce heat and simmer for 20 minutes. Remove from heat.

② Carefully pour the mixture into the blender. Have an adult help you. Blend until smooth.

③ Pour the mixture back into the large pot. Add the half-and-half, lemon juice, and nutmeg. Stir well. Add salt and pepper to taste. Over low heat, warm the soup to serving temperature.

④ Put the soup in serving bowls. **Garnish** with fresh basil.

1

2

3

4

# CRUNCHY
# Carrots & Raisins

This classic treat disappears at parties!

MAKES 8 SERVINGS

## INGREDIENTS

5 large carrots
1 cup raisins
¼ cup mayonnaise
2 tablespoons sugar
2 tablespoons milk

## TOOLS

grater
measuring cups
measuring spoons
mixing bowls
mixing spoon
2 spoons for tossing
whisk

**1**

① Grate the carrots. Use the largest holes on the grater. Keep grating until you have about 4 cups of grated carrots. Put them in a large bowl. Add the raisins.

② Make the dressing. Put the mayonnaise, sugar, and milk in a small bowl. Whisk together well.

③ Pour the dressing over the carrot and raisins. Toss the salad until the carrots and raisins are coated with dressing.

**2**

**3**

25

# Carrot Bake

This warm, cheesy side dish goes with any meal!

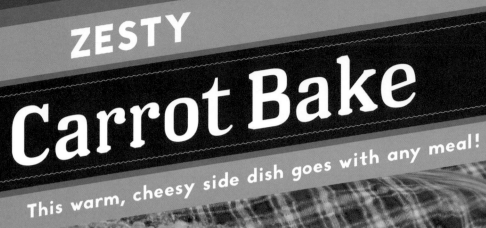

**MAKES 4 SERVINGS**

## INGREDIENTS

8 medium carrots,
peeled and sliced

¾ cup mayonnaise

2 tablespoons onion,
finely chopped

1 tablespoon horseradish

1 teaspoon salt

¼ teaspoon pepper

2 tablespoons
butter, softened

½ cup bread crumbs

½ cup grated
colby cheese

## TOOLS

peeler

cutting board

sharp knife

grater

8 × 8-inch baking dish

medium-sized pot

strainer

measuring cups

measuring spoons

mixing bowls

mixing spoon

1  Preheat the oven to 350 **degrees**. Grease the bottom and sides of the baking dish.

② Bring a medium-sized pot of water to a boil. Add the sliced carrots. Reduce the heat. Simmer for 2 minutes. Strain the carrots and place them in the bottom of the baking dish.

③ Put the mayonnaise, onion, horseradish, salt, pepper, and ⅓ cup water in a small bowl. Mix well. Pour the mixture over the carrots.

④ Mix the softened butter and bread crumbs together. Sprinkle it over the top of the carrots. Bake for 25 to 30 minutes. The top should be lightly **toasted.**

⑤ Remove the dish from the oven. Sprinkle the grated cheese on top. Return it to the oven for 2 to 3 minutes or until cheese is melted.

27

# COME-'N-GET-'EM

# Carrot Muffins

These tasty muffins are just as good as carrot cake!

MAKES 12 MUFFINS

## INGREDIENTS

⅔ cup raisins

1⅓ cups all-purpose flour

2 teaspoons baking powder

1¼ teaspoons baking soda

¾ teaspoon salt

¾ teaspoon ground cinnamon

2¾ eggs

⅔ cup vegetable oil

½ cup brown sugar

2 cups grated carrots

## TOOLS

measuring cups

mixing bowls

strainer

12-muffin tin

12 paper liners

measuring spoons

whisk

mixing spoon

grater

serving spoon

1. Put the raisins and 1⅓ cup warm water in a small bowl. Let **soak** for 15 minutes. Strain the raisins. Set them aside.

2. Preheat the oven to 350 **degrees**. Line the muffin tin with paper muffin liners.

3. Put the flour, baking powder, baking soda, salt, and cinnamon in a large bowl. Whisk together well. Set aside.

4. In a separate bowl, combine eggs, oil, and brown sugar. Whisk well. Add the egg mixture to the flour mixture. Mix just until moistened. Fold in carrots and raisins.

5. Use a serving spoon to put the carrot mixture in the muffin tin. Bake for 25 minutes. The muffins should rise and be golden brown on top. Let them cool for 30 minutes.

## WRAP IT UP!

Did you enjoy growing food from the earth? Are you a gifted cook with fresh ingredients? Fresh ingredients go a long way toward making food taste great. Ask the best chefs in the world. They'll tell you! Fresh ingredients are their secret ingredients!

By now you know that fresh food tastes great. Plus, it's good for the **environment**. Food from your garden doesn't require **transportation** or packaging. It isn't covered in harmful chemicals either!

So keep at it. Don't lose that green thumb! Think about your favorite foods. Can you grow them yourself? Chances are, you can. Check out the other books in this series. There may be a book about growing and cooking your favorite food!

# Glossary

**CITRUS** – a fruit such as an orange, lemon, or lime that has a thick skin and a juicy pulp.

**CONSISTENT** – always done the same way.

**CONTAINER** – something that other things can be put into.

**CULTIVATE** – to grow plants or crops.

**CYLINDER** – a solid shape with two parallel circles bound by a curved surface. A soda can is a cylinder.

**DEGREE** – the unit used to measure temperature.

**DISTURB** – to disorder or rearrange.

**ENVIRONMENT** – nature and everything in it, such as the land, sea, and air.

**FERTILIZER** – something used to make plants grow better in soil.

**GARNISH** – to decorate with small amounts of food.

**GERMINATE** – to begin to grow from a seed.

**MATURE** – to finish growing or developing.

**NUTRIENT** – something that helps living things grow. Vitamins, minerals, and proteins are nutrients.

**RECOMMEND** – to suggest or advise.

**SEEDLING** – a young plant that grew from a seed.

**SOAK** – to leave something in a liquid for a while.

**SOW** – to put seeds on or in soil so they will grow.

**SPROUT** – 1. to begin to grow. 2. a new plant growing from a seed.

**TOASTED** – cooked until it is dry and brown.

**TRANSPORTATION** – the act of moving people and things.

# Index